GENERATION Z

The Sleeping Giant Awakens...

WE HAVE THE POWER!

5/18/19

S.L. Daughtrey

To chris,

prayer without work is dead!
Just focus on your goal and work
toward striving for GREATNESS !

S.

Sharmaya Daughtrey

Published and Distributed By
Daughtrey Publishing House
Lakewood, California
Email: sdaughtrey@icloud.com

Packaging/Consulting
Professional Publishing House
1425 W. Manchester Ave. Ste B
Los Angeles, California 90047
323-750-3592
Email: professionalpublishinghouse@yahoo.com
www.Professionalpublishinghouse.com

Cover design: TWA Solutions
First printing March 2019
978-0578-46710-8
10987654321

For inquiry contact the publisher: sdaughtrey@icloud.com.

TABLE OF CONTENTS

The Constitution Of
Generation Z

We, the Young People of the United States of America, in order to form a more cohesive union, must stand on principles and work toward justice for all. We must ensure acceptance of our differences and strive to learn and grow in wisdom. We must stand on truth and challenge bigotry. Make no excuses, only changes, and strive to be the best that we can be to make way for a more humane and fair world.

E Pluribus Unum
Out of Many, One

BOYS, WHERE YOU AT?

In the fight against female brutality,
Boys, where you at?

1 out of 6 American women has been the victim of an
attempted, or completed rape, in her lifetime
Boys, where you at?

In the fight against gun violence,
Boys, where you at?

Statistics have shown between the years 1982 and
September 20, 2018, three mass shootings were initiated
by solo-female shooters. This is in contrast to 100 mass
shootings that were carried out by males.
Boys, where you at?

In a crowd of bullies
Boys, where you at?

In 2017, advocates tracked at least 29 deaths of transgender
people in the United States, due to fatal violence; and in
2018, there have already been at least 22 transgender people
who have been fatally shot, or killed by other violent means.
Boys, where you at?

In a divided nation
Boys, where you at?

Along the journey of becoming a man, on what issues will you fight for and take a stand?

Boys, where you at?

FOREWORD

by Christopher M. Murphy

The idea of a United States of America was born on July 4, 1776. Two-hundred and forty-three years later the idea has manifested into the world's oldest democracy. In an attempt to escape the brutal and harsh treatment of the English Monarchy, our Founding Fathers took a gamble on transforming 13 Colonies into a Republic. As text reveals, this original republic was far from inclusive. In 1789, the only Americans who possessed the right to vote were land-owning, white males. Through constant struggle, fight, petition and protest we have worked towards creating an inclusionary electorate protected by the United States Constitution. "The right of citizens of the United States, who are eighteen years of age or older, to vote shall not be denied or abridged by the United States or by any State on account of age." (*The Twenty-Sixth Amendment to the U.S. Constitution*).

Voting is the most precious right we have as members of the Republic. In fact, in the spring of 1957 Dr. Martin Luther King made it his central theme at the Prayer Pilgrimage for Freedom in Washington D.C.

"Give us the ballot, and we will no longer have to worry the federal government about our basic rights.

Give us the ballot, and we will no longer plead to the federal government for passage of an anti-lynching law; we will by the power of our vote write the law on the statute books of the South and bring an end to the dastardly acts of the hooded perpetrators of violence.

Give us the ballot, and we will transform the salient misdeeds of bloodthirsty mobs into the calculated good deeds of orderly citizens.

Give us the ballot, and we will fill our legislative halls with men of goodwill and send to the sacred halls of Congress men who will not sign a 'Southern Manifesto' because of their devotion to the manifesto of justice.

Give us the ballot, and we will place judges on the benches of the South who will do justly and love mercy, and we will place at the head of the southern states governors who will, who have felt not only the tang of the human, but the glow of the Divine.

Give us the ballot, and we will quietly and nonviolently, without rancor or bitterness, implement the Supreme Court's (Brown) decision of May seventeenth, 1954."

— Dr. Martin Luther King, Jr.
"Prayer Pilgrimage for Freedom" Speech
May 17, 1957

Those words spoken sixty-two years ago have never rung louder and truer than they do at this moment in history. In her book, *Generation Z . . . The Sleeping Giant Awakens...We Have the Power!*, Shanaya Daughtrey does a marvelous job of empowering her generation to stand up and recognize their unlimited potential. She calls on her peers to recognize the power of their collective voice to tackle the issues of our time. These issues include bullying, gun violence and gun rights, voting, elements of free speech, and sexual orientation and gender identity. In the grand scheme of things, these are issues that should be at the forefront of all conversations, regardless of one's generational identification. However, Shanaya does a masterful job of stressing the importance of Generation Z taking the lead in transforming our future. Shanaya weaves in our Constitution plus past historical events and figures as she lays out her concerns. As a teacher of Advanced Placement United States History, this comes as no surprise to me. I have known Shanaya for two years as a student and what has always impressed me is her understanding of the world around her and what her role could be as a student-leader. I love the title of Chapter 11, We Have the Power. I know that Shanaya truly believes this. Her honesty, passion, and conviction come out in her words. Shanaya is on an adventure to create real and positive change and is taking us along in her journey.

CHAPTER 1

We Are More Than Snapchat and Selfies

The Z's have awakened! Like the drop of water that tips over the bucket, the Florida school shooting at **Marjory Stoneman Douglas High School** was the drop that tipped over the bucket of water and woke us up. When brothers and sisters from the Florida school shooting stood up and said, "No more," they could not be silenced by negativity, they could not be silenced by their critics, who said it was not the time to speak on gun violence. Nor did they stop when they were told they were too young to involve themselves in the nature of politics and gun control.

The reality of it all is that school shootings have become a common occurrence. According to Time.com, "There have been 17 school shootings in 2018 alone, and 290 since 2013, shortly after Sandy Hook in New Town Connecticut."

We cried, we prayed and, we acknowledged the pain and losses that the families experienced. But, the wheels of justice continued to move slowly. **The National Rifle Association (NRA)** was not held accountable. Up until now—even though gun violence is still a current and reoccurring issue of our time—the youth have created a milestone that even adults were not willing to do. We were able to draw national attention to an issue that has been rampant ever since the mass school shooting at Columbine on April 20, 1999. We were courageous enough to speak out against the horrific acts that caused unnecessary losses, heartaches, and untimely deaths.

Resilient against the remarks of critics and politicians, the teenagers from Stoneman Douglas High school pushed so that their voices could be heard. For too long, we have looked passed this gun control issue as something that is going to disappear on its own, but now more than ever...IT KEEPS HAPPENING! The time of just wallowing in the shadows and complaining about what should be done is over. It is time now that WE GET UP AND ACTUALLY DO SOMETHING!

Our brothers and sisters have stepped up in a revolutionary way that is a key foundation in shaping and bettering our future. Despite what people—even our own parents might say—the youth is doing what the adults were hesitant to do, and that was speaking out against a higher power—the NRA—for a greater cause.

I respect the youth demographics of today and I am proud to be a part of it. Although we are in the age of technology and are perceived to be unaware of current economic and political issues, we are the ones that are actually fighting to be heard, along with using social media as a platform to voice our opinions.

Forced to be silenced is one thing but scared to be heard is another. Our brothers and sisters from the Florida school shooting were unafraid to voice their grievances and, in doing so, they started something bigger than themselves. They were like a powerful force of nature that rocked the country!

The fact of the matter is that if the victims that survived decided to just suffer in silence and let their tragedy be remembered as just a hashtag, then they would have never brought to light again the matter of gun control. It was as if they were shouting from the rooftop, "HELLO! TIMES UP! Stop avoiding the issue of gun control!"

The national walk-outs across the country and the televised march in Washington, D.C. that gained national attention from politicians and journalists, was just the beginning for something that would later on be regarded and recognized as the closest thing to change. It was the right beginning of something that should not fall to the wayside and be forgotten.

No! Gun control is an issue that must be in the forefront and constantly acknowledged. The victims, the survivors, and the parents of lost loved ones, will forever be haunted by the memory of what should not have happened...but did.

Where do you stand on the issue of gun control in America?

_____

_____

_____

_____

_____

_____

_____

_____

_____

_____

_____

_____

_____

_____

Generation Z

_____

_____

_____

_____

_____

_____

_____

_____

_____

_____

_____

_____

_____

_____

_____

_____

_____

_____

_____

_____

_____

_____

CHAPTER 2

Standing On The Shoulders

January 1, 1863, our 16th President of the United States, Abraham Lincoln, issued the Final Emancipation Proclamation. He declared all slaves forever free. And, on **December 6, 1865**, the **Thirteenth** Amendment was ratified. It outlawed slavery in the United States of America.

Revolution starts with the people. From the abolishment of slavery, from the Women's Suffrage Movement, to the Civil Rights Movement, they were all striving toward a better and more equal future that would not only benefit the minority that was fighting, but also define the line of what was right and wrong.

The origin of every revolution begins with issues that affect the rights, livelihood and lives of the people suffering; and when the torment gets intolerable, the thought of what

"I" or "we" can do to make things better, starts to stir in the minds of the oppressed. There was never a time in history where the people—no matter the race or gender—did not object to some form of rule, or law, that was seen as unjust. It is the way of the world and it is how our country came to be.

Today, many of us have a rainbow of friends: white, Black, Asian, Hispanic, gay, straight, transgender, Christian, Muslim, etc. However, less than **70** years ago, we could not swim together in the same pool, or play together at the same parks. In the southern states, segregation was the law of the land. But, let's not get it twisted. Racism permeated throughout the north, east, and west, of the United States of America too.

Our society is not a utopia. It has its obvious flaws and when the law that we expect to uphold our civil rights and liberties do not follow through, then it becomes our duty to decide whether to act upon the injustices and inequalities, or suffer in silence. We must be determined to exercise our inalienable rights and strive toward the difference that we want to see in the world in which we live.

Today, with all the marches and protests, who do you see at the forefront? Who do you see on the news and podiums speaking out? The youth! We are doing what the adults are now too complacent to do. Old politicians deflect from the real issues at hand. Today, we are the voice of the nation and we are the ones pushing for change. To quote Gandhi, **"Be the change you want to see in the world."** WE are the change agents that the world needs, and we are the push that is going to be a turning point in history.

With everything going on in politics, involving the NRA, in relation to the school shooting in Florida, the students stood their ground and said, "ENOUGH IS ENOUGH!" Through protest demonstrations and walk-outs and marches around the nation, we made it a key point that stricter gun control laws should be enforced. Since Columbine, leading all the way up to the Sandy Hook shooting, the discussion on gun control has been too loosely looked upon by our politicians. The time is now to put pressure on the people that have been voted into office to institute stricter gun control laws. It is a sad time in America, when a child has to receive active shooter drills during instructional class time. There should never be a time when a child should be scared to walk on school grounds, fearing that it might be their last. School should be the last place where fear of death overshadows the opportunity for learning.

Sadly, due to these past tragic events, when we watch the news and hear of a school shooter, the instance response is, "Again?" or "Another one?" These shootings are often seen as reoccurrences that are not accepted by society, but because of familiarity, it is almost normalized. The controversy involving gun control is linked to the NRA's belief that any regulation is a violation of the **Second Amendment**. The Second Amendment of the Constitution states, "A well-regulated Militia, being necessary to the security of a free State, the right of the people to keep and bear Arms, shall not be infringed."[1]

We are not trying to abolish the Second Amendment. However, we must address the call for stricter laws and background checks, and the type of assault rifles and the amount of ammunition that can be purchased. The issue on gun control is affecting the whole country and it is the fire that ignited many of the walk-out movements and marches, such as the one held in Washington, D.C, and schools around the nation. The time now has come to no longer look past these tragedies as a "sick incident," but to recognize the grim truth that this has happened too many times to NOT fuel some type of change toward the way guns are marketed and made so easily accessible.

As youth, we have the power to inculcate change in politics and make a mark that will long be noted in the future. We can say, when the adults did not step up, we did. The way to do this is exercising our right to vote. **WE MUST REGISTER TO VOTE WHEN WE REACH THE AGE OF 18**! This is the key to change; this is how we can determine the future for generations. The **vote** is a source for our power. It is so vital and makes such a difference, that some people overlook the fact that it is indeed a game changer that affects us, big or small.

---

[1] Compilation and Introduction, The Constitution of the United States of America with the Declaration of Independence, 2002 by Sterling Publishing Co., Inc.

The **2016** Presidential Election results left many people unhappy. Too bad, so sad. Many of the *unhappy* people did **not** vote. In the case of Trump versus Hilary Clinton, although she won the popular vote, she lost the Electoral College vote. She lost key states such as: Florida, Michigan, Ohio, Pennsylvania and Wisconsin. *If you do not know what the Electoral College voting system is, I challenge you to look up this antiquated system, and determine for yourself if it should be eliminated.* Voting is powerful, it levels the playing field; it gives us the chance to make our choice and when we do not take advantage of these opportunities, then we should not even bother to question why things did not go our way. Again, voting is our voice and, in order for us to ascertain a future that is centered toward our needs, we have to make sure we get out and vote and voice our opinion, because if we don't, then who will?

I know that as result of the voices, heard across the nation, from our brothers and sisters from Florida, a significant change in our fight for reasonable gun laws occurred. **This is what a CNN Politics page announced! "Exclusive: Trump administration to announce final bump stock ban." THIS IS A BIG F*$%# DEAL!** "Bump stocks gained national attention last year after a gunman in Las Vegas rigged his weapons with the devices to fire on concertgoers, killing 58 people. President Donald Trump vowed to outlaw the devices soon after the tragedy..."[2]

---

[2] CNN Politics, November 28, 2018.

Do you know that the right to vote was not always a right that every citizen had?

Does knowing that fact have an impact on how you view the importance of your vote?

_____

_____

_____

_____

_____

_____

_____

_____

_____

_____

_____

_____

_____

_____

_____

_____

_____

CHAPTER 3

Know Your History

In the past, voting was seen as almost a mere hope and dream for women and African Americans. In 1869—as a result of the South losing the Civil War—three new amendments were added to the Constitution. **On February 3, 1870,** the **Fifteenth** Amendment was ratified. It granted African American *men* the right to vote. This Amendment forbid discrimination in "access to the polls on the basis of race, color, or previous servitude."[3]

This was very important in the eyes of the abolitionists. They saw this as the most important right of citizenship for Black men, and at the end of reconstruction, Republicans

---

3 Compilation and Introduction, The Constitution of the United States of America with the Declaration of Independence, 2002 by Sterling Publishing Co., Inc.

knew that Democrats would regain control of state and local governments in the South. When this occurred, without access to the ballot, they concluded that their freedmen would lose their rights and also their only voice in government.

The key point in this is that their **voice** was their livelihood and without a say in the ballot, they were ultimately **powerless**. Even more so, back then, African Americans were given little to no opportunity to express their grievances about their place in society so when the **Fifteenth Amendment** was passed, it was a gateway toward change. Though still faced with adversity, a slither of hope was still in the crack of the door.

As for women, they were not given consideration to be allowed to vote. During the 1840s, the demand for **Women's Suffrage** sparked movement of women fighting for their rights. It was not until after a long and arduous fought series of votes in the U.S Congress and in state legislatures, that the **Nineteenth** Amendment, which was ratified August 18, 1920, stated that "the rights of citizens of the United States to vote shall not be denied or abridged by the United States or by any state on account of sex," became part of the U.S Constitution, **August 26, 1920.** [4]

---

[4] Compilation and Introduction, The Constitution of the United States of America with the Declaration of Independence, 2002 by Sterling Publishing Co., Inc.

This milestone in history did not come easy, and today, for women—let alone everyone that is a citizen of this country—to have the right to vote and voice their choice in the polls should not be taken lightly! The right to vote for any minority was once a fight that was long overdue and now it is a given. So, the choice between taking advantage and not taking advantage of your right to vote should be a no-brainer. **USE YOUR BRAIN!**

CHAPTER 4

Civics 101—*Unalienable Rights*

An **inalienable right** is a natural right that **cannot** be revoked, discarded, or ignored by any outside force. It is yours forever. The government, school officials, and even our parents cannot take it away from us. The **Constitution** says so. Thomas Jefferson, the principal author, who later became the third President of the United States of America, on March 4, 1801, wrote in the **Declaration of Independence** that all are "**endowed by their Creator with certain unalienable rights.**" And, "**We hold these Truths to be self-evident, that all men are created equal.**"[5]

This next line that I write, I implore that you imprint this in your memory, and bring it into remembrance when you

---

[5] www.civiced.org.

think to judge someone who does not fit into your realm of normal. All, and I repeat, ALL **have the unalienable right to "life, liberty, and the pursuit of happiness."**

On December 15, 1791, the state of Virginia ratified **10** proposed Constitutional Amendments, which added the **Bill of Rights** to the United States Constitution. The majority of us today do not know the amendments that were put into motion to guarantee certain unalienable rights of American citizens. After this chapter, you will know.

Below, are the **first ten** amendments, which are referred to as the **Bill of Rights.**

*Amendment I: Freedom of Religion, Speech, and the Press

"Congress shall make no law respecting an establishment of religion or prohibiting the free exercise thereof or abridging the freedom of speech or of the press."[6]

You have the right to practice the religion of your choosing, without being discriminated against. Let no one bully you about your religious beliefs and practices.

Your right to comment and post on Snapchat, Instagram, and Twitter is protected by this amendment. No one, not even

---

[6] Compilation and Introduction, The Constitution of the United States of America with the Declaration of Independence, 2002 by Sterling Publishing Co., Inc.

the President, has the power to stop you from speaking out on anything because we live in a democratic society. However, let's not go overboard. There are some limits. You cannot scream fire in an event setting, if there is no fire. And some of your postings may be deemed offensive and, come back to haunt you.

I will share with you two life-changing scenarios that really occurred:

Headline: **"Harvard Rescinds Admissions to 10 Students For Offensive Facebook Memes."**[7] The story: "At least 10 students accepted to Harvard had their offers rescinded after administrators discovered their offensive posts in a private, online Facebook messaging group…The Holocaust, child abuse, sexual assault, as well as posts that denigrated minority groups, were all fair game in the meme-focused private group chat….Harvard does not comment on individual applicants' admission statuses, but incoming students are explicitly told upon receiving an offer that behavior that brings into question their moral character can jeopardize their admission."[7]

I know that the students were devastated, and their parents were crushed. Harvard was their dream school. Harvard's acceptance rate is **5.2%**. Many students who aspire and dream of getting into Harvard have as much of a chance of getting into Harvard as Kanye West has of being President of the United States. Those 10 students got accepted, but

---

[7] www.forbes.com, June 5, 2017.

before they could pack their bags, step a foot on the campus, their dreams were shattered like glass. What is your dream school? Will your desire to get into the school of your dream be derailed because of a post that you made on social media?

Kevin Hart, a famous comedian, excitedly tweeted what he deemed an opportunity of a lifetime. "For years, I have been asked if I would ever Host the Oscars and my answer was always the same…I said it would be an opportunity of a lifetime…I am so happy to say that this day has finally come for me to host the Oscars. I am blown away simply because this has been on my goal list for a long time."

Unfortunately, the goal imploded when the history of his homophobic tweets, made nine years ago, resurfaced.

Headline: **"Kevin Hart's History of Homophobic Tweets, Jokes, Resurfaces As Oscar's Gig Is Announced."**[8] "The Academy Awards' decision was blasted as a 'middle finger' to the LGBTQ community, given the comedian's past remarks." **This is the result of his past actions.**

Subsequently, Kevin Hart tweeted, "I have made the choice to step down from hosting this year's Oscars… This is because I do not want to be a distraction on a night that should be celebrated by so many amazing talented artists. I sincerely apologize to the LGBTQ community for my insensitive words from my past."

---

[8] www.huffingtonpost.com, Curtis M. Wong, December 6, 2018.

Is an apology ever enough? Should we ever forgive past deeds, no matter how big or small? Did Kevin Hart commit an unforgivable act?

_____

_____

_____

_____

_____

_____

_____

_____

_____

_____

_____

_____

_____

_____

_____

_____

_____

_____

_____

_____

_____

_____

Think about this question, and write your answer.

Are we becoming so politically correct, that we are diminishing our right of freedom of speech?

_____

_____

_____

_____

_____

_____

_____

_____

_____

_____

_____

_____

_____

_____

_____

_____

_____

_____

_____

*Amendment II: The Right to Bear Arms

"The right of the people to keep and bear Arms, shall not be infringed." [9]

A lot of controversy comes with this amendment because of the prevalent and reoccurring mass shootings. The same questions have been asked and hardly answered. Why aren't some people prone to background checks before purchasing guns? Such as, individuals who were hospitalized for suicidal or homicidal thoughts, individuals with violent criminal histories, or individuals that are reported by friends, families, or school officials for verbally expressing or posting on social media, threats of harming others.

What are we doing about **bullying**, which can lead to tragic outcomes when a fed-up victim has access to a gun and makes a decision that will negatively impact his/her life forever? We must seriously ask ourselves, "Why do individuals need to stockpile massive amounts of ammunition and bump stocks for high powered weapons, as if they are preparing for war? How many more innocent people have to die before we tighten gun control laws? These are appropriate questions that deserve answers, but where are the answers?

---

[9]Compilation and Introduction, The Constitution of the United States of America with the Declaration of Independence, 2002 by Sterling Publishing Co., Inc.

If you had an opportunity to work on gun control legislation, what changes, *if any,* would you make? Why?

*Amendment III: The Housing of Soldiers

In any time during peace, this amendment protects tenants of houses from having to house soldiers without their consent.[10]

In other words, no military personnel out of the blue can come into your house and say, "We are soldiers and we're going to be staying here for a while. What's for dinner?" This Amendment applied back to the Revolutionary War when American citizens in colonies were required to provide British Soldiers with housing and food.

*Amendment IV: Protection from Unreasonable Searches and Seizures

This amendment protects us from being unreasonably searched.[10]

All those people that we have seen on the news being stopped and frisked at will by the police, were stripped of their rights, and violated. It was done on a frequent basis to Black and brown people in New York City. "In **Floyd v. The City of New York,** decided on August 12, 2013, US District Court Judge Shira Scheindlin ruled the Stop and Frisk had

---

[10] Compilation and Introduction, The Constitution of the United States of America with the Declaration of Independence, 2002 by Sterling Publishing Co., Inc.

been used in an unconstitutional manner and directed the police to adopt a written policy to specify where such stops are authorized."[11]

This **abominable** practice has finally been put to rest. It took a lawsuit to stop this violation of our protected right. **FLASH!** This violation did not just happen in New York City—they just took it to a whole new level. This type of violation has happened, and continues to happen, across our Nation to mostly the Black and brown. Again, that is why it is vital to know your rights, and do something about it when your rights are violated. Do so in a nonviolent manner. For example, protest, sue, or make a formal complaint.

*Amendment V: Protection of Rights to Life, Liberty, and Property

Aside from rights to Life, Liberty, and Property, there is a lot that falls under this amendment. Such as "no person shall be held to answer for a capital, or otherwise infamous crime, unless on a presentment" (presentment is another word for presentation or display) "or indictment of a Grand Jury, except in cases arising in the land or naval forces, or in the Militia, when in actual service in time of war or public danger; nor shall any person be subject for the same offense to be **twice put in jeopardy** (*double jeopardy*) of life or limb; nor shall

---

[11]Wikipedia.com

be compelled in any criminal case to be a witness against himself, nor be deprived of life, liberty, or property without due process of law, nor shall private property be taken for public use without just compensation." [12]

*Amendment VI: Rights of Accused Persons in Criminal Cases

This amendment applies to all criminal prosecutions, the accused person has the right to a speedy trial by "an impartial jury of the state and district wherein the crime shall have been committed, which district shall have been previously ascertained; by law, and to be informed of the nature and cause of the accusation; to be confronted with the witnesses against him; to have compulsory process for obtaining witnesses in his favor; and to have the assistance of counsel in his favor." [12]

For example, if a crime is committed in Los Angeles, then that person has a right to have his trial in Los Angeles.

*Amendment VII: Rights in Civil Cases

"In suits at common law, where the value of controversy shall exceed twenty dollars, the right of trial by jury shall

---

[12] Compilation and Introduction, The Constitution of the United States of America with the Declaration of Independence, 2002 by Sterling Publishing Co., Inc.

be preserved, and no **fact tried by a jury shall be otherwise reexamined** in any court of the United States than according to the rules of the common law." [12]

Being a juror is very important, and it is a duty that carries great responsibility and weight. So, I strongly advise, when you reach adulthood status, not to throw away a jury summons. It is an honor to serve on a jury. And, we do not have enough minority representation because, many people throw away or disregard a jury summons.

*Amendment VIII: Excessive Bail, Fines, and Punishment Forbidden

"Excessive bail shall not be required, nor excessive fines imposed, nor cruel and unusual punishments inflicted."[13]

When I express to you to do the best that you can in school, so that you can get an education that will prepare you to be a productive member of society, I do not want to sound like a nagging parent. I want to be considered a friend that cares. A lack of education, poor job skills, equals a potential life of poverty. Poverty with no good options, or alternatives, can potentially drive someone to engage in criminal activity. Getting locked up can be very expensive for you, or your

---

[13] Compilation and Introduction, The Constitution of the United States of America with the Declaration of Independence, 2002 by Sterling Publishing Co., Inc.

parent(s). In order to get out of jail, your parent(s) may have to drain their savings, mortgage their home, or use your college savings.

Bail, in many cases, cannot be made because of the cost. I was shocked when I read this. "On any given day in 2015, roughly 700,000 people were locked up in local jails. The majority of them had **not** been **convicted** of a crime." [14]

So, if you are hanging out with your friends and someone in the group commits an alleged crime, the police can decide to take everyone in the group at the scene where the event took place, to jail. **Now get this**, "After an arrest—wrongful or not—a person's ability to leave jail and return home to fight the charges depends on **money**. That's because, in most states, people are required to pay cash bail. This is despite the fact that they are presumed innocent and have **not** been **convicted** of a crime."[15] "A money bail is a specific amount of money that is posted "so that the suspect can be released from pre-trial detention" [16]

Now that you know this information, I hope it will give you the insight to avoid situations that may cost you your freedom. And your designer outfits will consist of orange jumpsuits with numbers on the back; and your gold chains

---

[14] www.acly.org, bail reform.

[15] www.aclu.org, the truth about bail: it doesn't work.

[16] www.wikipedia.com, bail.

and watches will be substituted for handcuffs and shackles. Enough said.

News Alert! California has become the **first** state to **abolish** money bail! Abolishing money bail is such a big deal because "Defendants who can't afford bail may spend long periods awaiting trial for minor offenses...Bail also pushes many to plead guilty rather than wait indefinitely in jail for trial."[17]

Note: If you tend to run with the criminal element and live in another state, you may want to consider moving to California when you turn 18. Just saying.

Taking the place of money bail in California, will be **"pretrial assessments that will classify people's risk of offending while free."**[17]

*Amendment IX: Other Rights Kept By The People

"The enumeration in the Constitution of certain rights shall not be construed to deny or disparage others retained by the people." [18]

---

[17] www.washingtonpost.com.

[18]Compilation and Introduction, The Constitution of the United States of America with the Declaration of Independence, 2002 by Sterling Publishing Co., Inc.

An example of another right kept by the people that fall outside of the Constitution would be any person having the right to control what happens to their body and making their own medical decisions.

*Amendment X: Undelegated Powers Kept By The States And The People

"The powers not delegated to the United States by the Constitution, nor prohibited by it to the states, are reserved to the states respectively, or to the people."[19] In the next paragraphs below, I give an example of the Tenth Amendment.

FYI. To give you a clearer understanding of what this amendment means, I will discuss a state law that most of us are now familiar with. Many people, young and old, celebrated the passage of medical and recreational use of Marijuana a.k.a. Weed. According to the Sacramento Bee, you are allowed one ounce of Marijuana, or eight grams of Cannabis concentrate. However, do not get too excited because this law is not applicable in all states. And, currently it is still a **violation** of Federal Law to possess weed. The **political party** that is in power determines how strongly that Federal Law will be upheld.

---

[19]Compilation and Introduction, The Constitution of the United States of America with the Declaration of Independence, 2002 by Sterling Publishing Co., Inc.

As of the year 2018, Alaska, California, Colorado, Maine, Massachusetts, Michigan, Nevada, Oregon, Vermont, Washington State, Washington, D.C, are the only states that permit the use of recreational and medical marijuana. So if you plan on becoming a police officer, a fireman, a registered nurse, a teacher, a physician, pharmacist, pilot, professional athlete, etc., let this paragraph sink into your brain. Federal Law **supersedes** State Law. You will be breaking federal law and could risk losing your job and or license if you test positive, or post on social media a picture of yourself smoking weed, and it is revealed to your employer or school. Remember, what happens in Vegas, does not always stay in Vegas!

Let me take this a step further. If you get caught smoking weed in Alabama, Georgia, Louisiana, Tennessee, or TEXAS, you could end up getting serious jail time! Don't play!

For our transgender brothers and sisters, the gender-neutral bathroom law was created to respect their rights for equality. There is still much work to be done. Below is a list of states that have gender-neutral restroom laws for bars, restaurants, stores…wherever the law is effective.

1. **California**, effective March 1, 2017 "Any business establishment having a single-use bathroom—one having no more than one water closet and one urinal

with a locking mechanism controlled by the user—must identify that bathroom as all gender." [20]

2. **Washington, D.C.** "Municipal Regulations 4-802 has adopted a similar regulation that requires single-stall restrooms to have gender-neutral signage." [21] The state even has their own hashtag that coincides gender-neutral bathroom regulations. **"#safebathroomDC, encourages citizens to actively contribute to making all single-stall restrooms into gender-neutral."** [20]

3. **New York City**, March 2016, Mayor Bill de Blasio, "signed into law that restaurants, bars, and other public places in New York City with single-stall restrooms are required to replace 'men' and 'women' signage with gender neutral signage." [20]

4. **Philadelphia**, in January 2016, the state's gender-neutral bathroom bill went into effect. This law was an add-on to the previous existing law, specifying transgender individuals being able to use **whichever** bathroom the person is most comfortable using. "The January 2016 law required all local businesses with single-occupancy restrooms update the signage to indicate a gender-neutral bathroom within 90 days, or face a fine ranging $75 to $2,000."[20]

---

[20] www.mrllp.com, Health and Safety Code 118600

[21] www.milrose.com

Progress has been made, but the fight for equality continues.

Now, today, with prominent issues such as voter suppression across some parts of the United States, The Fifteenth and **Nineteenth Amendments** are more relevant than ever. The **Nineteenth Amendment, which was ratified on August 18,1920**, states: "The right of citizens of the United States to vote shall not be denied or abridged by the United States or by any state on account of sex,"[22] was added in regards to women initially not having the right to vote, unlike men.

Today, men and women of all color can vote and be a part of the democracy that was created to ensure the fair distribution of power. And that, today, is needed now more than ever. We, as a people, more so the youth, have an obligation to fill the polls and vote on issues that affect us and our daily lives in the long haul. In order for change to happen, we cannot hesitate in turbulent times; we must do the exact opposite and engage in the rally of wanting to be heard.

I hope that you found this chapter on the Bill of Rights engaging. And, I hope that you will continue on the journey

---

[22] Compilation and Introduction, The Constitution of the United States of America with the Declaration of Independence, 2002 by Sterling Publishing Co., Inc.

of furthering your knowledge about **The Constitution of The United States of America.** Despite the flaws, we are a great Nation!

How does knowing your rights empower you?

CHAPTER 5

Every Great Leader Needs A Push

Behind every great movement in history, there was a leader that was venerated because of their courage to go against the norm and aim toward something greater in the name of change for future generations and the people of that time. What I'm about to share with you are glimpses of the lives of great individuals who made an impact on the world in which we live in today. After reading about these individuals, I truly hope that you will further read and study on the depths of these special people who made great contributions and sacrifices so that we may have an equal and just world for everyone.

We all have our special gifts and talents. I recall hearing this profound quote from Kevin Durant, "Hard work beats talent, when talent fails to work hard." These individuals not only worked hard, but they believed that they could make a difference.

Sir Winston Churchill, Prime Minister of England, was a multifaceted giant. He was a former soldier, a statesman, an orator, and a writer. He is described in the history books as a defender of democracy. He came from the depths of obscurity to lead Great Britain out of the clutches of Adolf Hitler. He was a man that was not afraid to fail. He did not let past failures stop him from moving forward. And when Great Britain and the United States of America were on the brink of falling to pieces because of the threat of Nazi Germany and the rise of Adolf Hitler, Sir Churchill provided an unparalleled strength of leadership. He was able to effectively negotiate with foes such as Joseph Stalin, Communist Dictator of Russia, and allies, such as Franklin D. Roosevelt, President of the U.S.

He was known to be courageous in the face of adversity. Before his comeback during World War II, Churchill was a mere obscurity in the bustling background of Britain. After making a bad decision in World War I, Churchill left the political arena for over a decade. However, I truly believe he felt that if given another chance, one day, he would not fail again. From my study of Sir Churchill, I can say with certainty that he believed that when the time was right, he was going to get a chance to do something great, not for himself, but for the world in which he was a part of.

Like I previously mentioned, not every leader started off as a great leader. But, overcoming obstacles amidst dire circumstances, was the push that propelled them to greatness.

It took the rise of Nazi Germany for people to reconsider Winston Churchill as the potential national leader that could lead Britain out of the darkness and away from peril.

On May 10, 1940, Winston Churchill became the prime minister of Britain. When **"World War II began to rise out of the darkness of Nazi Germany,"**[23] Churchill was not fearful but instead prepared. After becoming prime minister, he later wrote, **"I felt… that all my past life had been but a preparation for this hour and for this trial."**[24] He admitted that at a time so dark and worrisome, he was prepared to take on the threat that he knew was coming. And, because of his stern determination, his unconfined energy, and his faith in his ability, he was able to succeed.

Now, consider **Mahatma Gandhi**. Although he is best known for his leadership in the Indian Independence Movement against Britain, spanning over two decades from 1920 to 1947, let us not forget. Just like Martin Luther King, Jr., Gandhi was also discriminated against just because of the color of his skin. Racism is everywhere. It permeates across

---

[23] www.youtube.com, Winston Churchill Biography

[24] IWM.org.uk/How Churchill Led Britain to Victory in The Second World War, James Taylor.

continents, yet the evils of racism can only succeed when *"good"* people say or do nothing.

Upon his visit to **South Africa** in 1893, Gandhi was confronted with discrimination. Like bus segregation in the United States' South—where Blacks were forced to sit in the back, or forced to give up their seat to a white passenger—Gandhi was not allowed to sit next to any white passengers while traveling by train. On June 7, 1893, Gandhi was forcibly removed for sitting in a "white only" section of the train. Because of his skin tone, he was treated differently and unfairly. And even while being beaten after his refusal to give up his seat, he did not fight back. That is not an easy thing to do.

After such a traumatic event, how could one not want to make a difference, and try and change the harsh bigotry of the world? So, instead of going back to India right away, he stayed in South Africa for 21 years and protested against the racial discrimination that Indians faced. Gandhi pivoted in the direction of nonviolence, a method that he believed could get a valid point across, while at the same time, showing no ambition toward hostility, or violence. During his time in South Africa, he developed a strategy that coincided with nonviolent civil disobedience called *satyagraha*, also known as the "truth force." [25]

---

[25] Gandhi.southafrica.net

From the time Gandhi first implemented nonviolent civil disobedience in South Africa, during a time where the "resident Indian communities were struggling for civil rights,"[26] he saw this as a continuing method that could benefit his people in the fight for liberation under Britain's rule. When he returned to India in **1915**, he focused on **"organizing peasants, farmers, and urban laborers to protest against excessive land-tax and discrimination."** [26]

As I said before, **revolution starts with the people.** No matter how poor, no matter how uneducated, no matter what color you are, when people get sick and tired of being sick and tired, they will either rise up and fight for change, or perish under the weight of oppression.

Gandhi accomplished great things because he was persistent and he persevered. He was also determined. I call it the **PPD** effect. When those forces are put into motion, you will succeed. Gandhi was beaten and imprisoned. Opposing forces tried to stop Gandhi. But because he had set into motion the PPD effect, he went on to accomplish freeing India from British rule in 1947.

Next, let's study **Dr. Martin Luther King, Jr.**, a relentless civil rights activist, a pastor, an advocate and leader, who followed Gandhi's way of nonviolence. He thought it not to be "a form of political theatre to move people into

---

[26] en.wikipedia.org/Mahatma Gandhi

sympathy with the downtrodden," but a means for compelling mass movements that were noticeable and effective. Dr. King idolized Gandhi and his stance on confronting issues without the need for violence. His philosophy, piggybacking off of Gandhi's, was influential and world renowned. Even more so, today, Dr. King is celebrated due to the fact that his work and efforts didn't go unnoticed and his dream didn't die with him.

In his first book, *Stride Toward Freedom*, Dr. King wrote of six principles that were fundamental tenets of his philosophy toward nonviolence:

*"**Principle One**: Nonviolence is a way of life for courageous people.*

It is active nonviolent resistance to evil. It is aggressive spiritually, mentally and emotionally.

*"**Principle Two**: Nonviolence seeks to win friendship and understanding. The end result of nonviolence is redemption and reconciliation. The purpose of nonviolence is the creation of the Beloved Community.*

*"**Principle Three**: Nonviolence seeks to defeat injustice, not people. Nonviolence recognizes that evildoers are also victims and are not evil people. The nonviolent resister seems to defeat evil, not people.*

*"**Principle Four**: Nonviolence holds that suffering can educate and transform. Nonviolence accepts suffering without retaliation. Unearned suffering is redemptive and has tremendous educational and transforming possibilities.*

*"**Principle Five**: Nonviolence chooses love instead of hate. Nonviolence resists violence of the spirit as well as the body. Nonviolent love is spontaneous, unmotivated, unselfish and creative,*

*"**Principle Six**: Nonviolence believes that the universe is on the side of justice. The nonviolent resister has deep faith that justice will eventually win. Nonviolence believes that God is a God of justice."* [27]

Centered around Gandhi's teachings, these iconic and fundamental tenets were incorporated throughout all of his demonstrations and marches. They were essential in what he was trying to accomplish during the Civil Rights Movement. Instead of trying to use the method of **"By Any Means Necessary,"** which was the ideology of the great Malcom X, Dr. King went down a different path that ultimately and eventually changed The United States as we know it.

Throughout Dr. King's crusade toward equality and the betterment of African Americans, he faced criticism even from his own people. But regardless of the adversity that was hurdled his way, he never doubted that what he was doing wasn't right and what he was trying to accomplish wasn't worth the sacrifices. If you try to please all the people, all the time, you will **NOT** get anything accomplished!

At the forefront in politics, during Dr. King's journey toward equality and civil rights for African Americans,

---

[27] thekingcenter.org

President John F. Kennedy was instrumental, alongside Dr. King, that helped initiate the goal that Dr. King was fighting so hard to accomplish. On June 11, 1963, President Kennedy delivered his **"Report to the American People on Civil Rights"** speech. In his speech, the president offered legislation that would later on become the **Civil Rights Act of 1964** and conveyed civil rights as being a moral issue and proclaimed that racial equality was a just cause. Not only was it a just cause, it was a mandate in our Constitution. Racial equality for all was long overdue.

Blacks were tired of the disrespect and degradation just because of the color of their skin, tired of having to suffer in silence and tired of being punished and jailed when they tried to be heard. Yes, President Kennedy, it was long overdue!

"Cautious at first because he was worried that such drastic measures would alienate legislators in the heavily segregated South,"[28]—Kennedy finally came to the conclusion of offering stronger support for civil rights. In truth, **he needed a push** and motivation to do so. It wasn't until African Americans became more and more impatient about the lack of social progress and **"the rising militancy of the civil rights movement that agitated white Americans and further caused deterioration that was looked down**

---

[28]en.m.wikipedia.org/Report to the American People on Civil Rights

upon from abroad "[29] —that ultimately forced the president's hand in supporting the civil rights movement. Actually, it was President Lyndon Johnson who signed the Civil Rights Bills, because Kennedy was assassinated on 11-22-63. **"Lyndon Johnson Signs Civil Rights Act of 1964.** The **Civil Rights Act of 1964,**(7-2-64) the most sweeping **civil rights** legislation since Reconstruction, prohibited racial discrimination in employment and education, and outlawed segregation in public facilities."

Resilient, motivated, and dedicated. These three words are attributable to **Nelson and Winnie Mandela.** Fueled by the racial inequity that was exhibited throughout all South Africa, they worked diligently, leading protests, rallies, and boycotts to end the apartheid that oppressed the people of their country.

Similar to Jim Crow, the apartheid that occurred in South Africa for **50** years, was an abhorrent abomination **that "encouraged state repression of Black African, Coloured, and Asian South Africans for the benefit of the nation's minority white population."**[30] In a racially divided country, liberation from the cuffs of segregation and bigotry was all that people could hope for. So many lives lost in the fight for justice, so many brick walls blockading the way toward freedom; it was more than a time of great turmoil, it was a time of extreme suffering.

---

[29] en.m.wikipedia.org/Report to the American People on Civil Rights

[30] en.m.wikipedia.org/Apartheid

Nelson Mandela, former president of South Africa, was a crusader for justice and equality. He was the leader of both peaceful protests and arm resistant protests. His actions with the African National Congress (ANC), which consisted of sit-ins, boycotts, strikes, and other forms of civil disobedience—coincided with their goal to attain full citizenship for all South Africans. Their efforts were deemed treasonous and resulted in multiple arrests. Mandela never feared incarceration because what he was fighting for was bigger than a jail cell. Even within the walls of prison, his efforts in trying to end the apartheid never ceased. He was able to surreptitiously smuggle out political statements and a draft of his autobiography, *Long Walk to Freedom*, which was published five years after he got out of prison.

Where there is a will, there is a way. The government's effort in trying to silence the work of Mandela and put an end to what he and the people of South Africa were striving to achieve, did not work. You can lock up a man with a cause, but you can't lock up the cause with the man. Mandela was given a life sentence by the court for his efforts of resistance. He ultimately served 27 years.

There was only so much that he could do from prison, and that's where **Winnie Mandela** comes in. She kept the movement alive and growing! Her unabating efforts and sacrifices that she made to keep the movement alive is so often overlooked and belittled. Winnie Mandela was a woman of strength. She did not let the weight of oppression silence her voice. Prior to their engagement, Winnie was already actively involved in the politics of the Anti-Apartheid Movement, and when Nelson Mandela was no longer able to be in the forefront of the movement—due to his confinement in prison—Winnie was there to step in, step up, and take over the responsibilities that were once her husband's.

Known as the "**Mother of the Nation**" to many black South Africans, she endured the "**uncompromising opponent of the then predominant racial segregation system.**"[31] She was forced into exile in 1976 to the border town of Brandfort, South Africa, where she was placed under house arrest for the duration of nine years. Her being on house arrest was the government's way of trying to isolate and break her. She described the experience as "**alienating and heart-wrenching.**"[31] What made it so unbearable was the fact that she understood the language of the people of Brandfort, but she couldn't speak it. So she was put in a position to fail and crumble, and no longer seek an end to the apartheid system.

Isolation and heartache were not enough to keep her silent, or kill her spirit. Winnie Mandela—despite her own individual pain and suffering—continued to speak out against the racially unjust system.

---

[31] Aljazeera.com/ Who was South Africa's Winnie Mandela?

She exemplified true attributes of a force to be reckoned with, and her unyielding pursuit to freedom was undaunted by the discriminatory racial system that was set in place to keep people of color at the bottom, abused, and silent. As Nelson Mandela described her, after announcing their separation, "She endured the persecutions heaped upon by her by the government with exemplary fortitude and never wavered from her commitment to the struggle for freedom."[32] I truly believe Winnie Mandela's role in the Anti-Apartheid Movement was bigger than what she is accredited for. What Winnie accomplished while Nelson Mandela was imprisoned, gave him a stronger platform after his release.

Sharing about great leaders from our past, and how their contributions heavily influenced our world today, we see how our most prominent leaders made their presence known and voices ring throughout the country. Leaders that instilled change upon politicians, pushed for civil innovation between races, and gained advocates along the way, then ultimately made their mark in history.

Guess what, **Generation Zs?** Many of the leaders were students. John Lewis, the 79-year-old, U.S. Congressman, was a student leader in the Civil Rights Movement.

I am now going to shift and discuss with you glimpses into the lives of some of our great leaders of our generation,

---

[32] Aljazeera.com/ Who was South Africa's Winnie Mandela?

leaders that are pursuing justice in the name of change and equality. There are always going to be people who are bright in spirit and strong in will; willing to sacrifice and go above and beyond to protect and fight for the rights that we have as a people. The world is filled with valiant people who want to make a difference and who want to be heard.

The courageous leaders of today must not forget the lessons that we learned from the great and powerful leaders of yesterday.

I recall my mother's comment one day when I referred to her as "**old school**."

She said, "You can learn from the generation that you now call old." She then went into one of her dialogues. She said, "Shanaya, remember when I went on a cruise, and described to you how magnificent the ship was? Well, someone, centuries ago, designed a blueprint for a boat that could cross continents. Fast-forward across the continuum of time. We now have fleets of amazing ships because a blueprint that was left from our past demonstrated that it could be done."

I thought about those words. We must not sever the ties with those that came before us. We must stand on their shoulders and continue to grow. **We must be determined to build bridges, not walls of separation.**

CHAPTER 6

New Leaders, Who Dis?

You don't have to be rich or famous, or born into a political dynasty, to get elected to the United States Congress. You just have to be someone with a strong sense of purpose and a strong belief that you can do it. Alexandria believed she could do it! **Alexandria Ocasio-Cortez,** the **youngest** person ever elected to the United States House of Representatives, comes from a working-class family. She was born in the Bronx, New York City, October 13, 1989. She graduated from Boston University, Cum Lade in 2011, with a bachelor's degree in International Relations and a minor in Economics. After graduating college, she moved back home and had to work as a bartender and waitress to earn a living. Following the death of her father, she and her mother struggled to keep their house from foreclosing. She could have felt helpless and hopeless after facing such devastation, and gave up, but she didn't. She continued to work hard and became politically active.

Coming from a working-class family, she understood the value of hard work and education. During 2016, Ocasio-Cortez worked on the Bernie Sanders's 2016 presidential campaign. After the general election, she traveled across America in her car.

One of the places she decided to go to was Standing Rock, North Dakota, an Indian Reservation, to protest with the Native Americans that were in jeopardy of losing their land to a big oil company that wanted to drill for oil. This would also have a very negative impact on the environment. She became so enthralled with their purpose and their determination to fight the injustice, that she no longer believed that you had to have money, power, and social connections to make a difference and, become an elected official to represent her community. She now believed that she could organize and work for her own community to improve their lives. SHE WON! She beat an incumbent that had held the seat for decades.

Every voice matters. It doesn't matter if you are **gay, straight, lesbian, bisexual, or transgender**. You should not be denied anything in life because of the way you identify yourself. As stated in our **Constitution, "We hold these truths to be self-evident, that all men are created equal, that they are endowed by their Creator with certain inalienable**

Rights, that among these are Life, Liberty, and the Pursuit of Happiness." [33]

In our society today, we have people fighting to uphold the rights of **ALL** people.

Chad Griffin is one of these people. His origination in politics began when he started volunteering for the Bill Clinton presidential campaign. This volunteer work led to a position in the White House Press Office. Actively advocating for same sex marriage, Griffin founded the **American Foundation for Equal Rights (AFER)** to overturn the 2008 passage of Proposition 8, which obstructed the recognition of same-sex marriage. AEFR's challenge, *Perry v. Brown*, which "were a series of United States federal court cases that legalized same-sex marriage in the state of California...was ultimately successful following a decision by the United States Supreme Court in June 2013." [34]

Griffin's hard work gained him appointment of president of **the Human Rights Campaign, the largest LGBT rights organization in the United States.**

The contribution that he made to society impacted the lives of so many in our country and it was rooted from his passion to right a wrong that was not only unconstitutional,

---

[33]Compilation and Introduction, The Constitution of the United States of America with the Declaration of Independence, 2002 by Sterling Publishing Co., Inc.

[34] https://en.m.wikipedia.org/wiki/Chad_Griffin.

but unfair to those who choose who they want to love and identify themselves as to how they want to be seen.

Kim Kardashian, a celebrity, an entrepreneur, and an activist, has broken barriers using her celebrity status to promote social justice for prison reform. Her efforts, at the time of writing this book, have led to three individuals getting their life sentences commuted. The first high profile case that she took on, and met with President Donald Trump to discuss granting a pardon to, was the case of **Alice Marie Johnson,** who received 21 years for a first-time, nonviolent drug offense. That meeting with the president was pivotal in getting Ms. Johnson pardoned.

Her most recent breakthrough was advocating on the behalf of **Cyntoia Brown** to be released from prison. Kim Kardashian asked Governor Bill Haslam of Tennessee to review her case and consider granting her clemency. Cyntoia Brown was a poor black teenage girl with no family support, who was under the control of a vicious pimp. She was caught up in the horrors of sex trafficking. At the age of 16, she was convicted for killing her rapist. She had inadequate representation during her trial and ultimately, experienced a miscarriage of justice that changed the course of her life. She served 15 years of a life sentence before being granted clemency.

Kim Kardashian's efforts were not in vain. Cyntoia Brown will be released on August 7, 2019 on parole supervision. Kim

Kardashian, an unlikely **shero** for prison reform, is changing lives, one release at a time. **Go Kim K!**

Michelle Alexander, author of *The New Jim Crow,* is one of our leaders of today. She is a civil rights advocate and was a law clerk for U.S Supreme Court Justice Harry Blackmun and for Chief Judge Abner Mikva on the United States Court of Appeals for the D.C. Circuit.

In her book, *The New Jim Crow,* Alexander focuses on the incarceration of African American men. **"She considers the scope and impact of this current law enforcement, legal and penal activity to be comparable with that of the Jim Crow laws of the 19ᵗʰ and 20ᵗʰ centuries."**[35] For those who may not be familiar with **Jim Crow laws,** Jim Crow laws were state and local laws that enforced racial segregation in the southern portion of the United States. These **laws "mandated the segregation of public schools, public places, and public transportation, and the segregation of restrooms, restaurants, and drinking fountains for whites and blacks."**[36] The **"separate but equal"** legal doctrine was upheld by the U.S Supreme Court's in **1896.** "As a body of law, **Jim Crow institutionalized economic, educational, and social disadvantage for African Americans."** [37]

---

[35] en.wikipedia.org/wiki/Michelle_Alexander

[36] https://en.wikipedia.org/wiki/JimCrowlaws

[37] en.wikipedia.org/wiki/Michelle_Alexander

Side Note—Who is Jim Crow? Jim Crow was not a politician, but a fictional character that was created by a man named Thomas Dartmouth Rice. Rice portrayed the character Jim Crow as a slave and would darken his face, speak with an "exaggerated and distorted imitation of African American Vernacular English," [38] and sing and dance and prance around the stage in a manner that was very derogatory toward African Americans. Although Rice was not the first white comedian to perform caricatures about blackface, he was the most popular entertainer of the time. "As a result of Rice's success, 'Jim Crow' became a common stage persona for white comedians' blackface portrayals of African Americans." [38]

Many of you who may be thinking Jim Crow Laws are the past, and what does that have to do with me today? I can go where I want to go, and I can eat where I choose to eat, and I can have an eclectic group of friends. **Expand your mind, and think free labor, and profits.**

Michelle Alexander's book is not only informative, but the data revealed can be used as a powerful tool for change. Think about this. In **California**, the state in which I live, spends **$8,667** per year for each college **student**, yet, it spends on an average **$50,000** for each **prisoner**. And get this. In the past 30 years, my state, has built **one** new college campus, but **20** new prisons. If you attend a community college, today, it could

---

[38] ferris.edu/Jim Crow Museum

possibly take you three to four years to get an Associate's Degree because there are not enough resources available to handle the needs of the students.

For example, there is a need for additional classes and professors. **What does your state spend?** Look it up. You will be as shocked as I was when I discovered the information.

The next change agent on my list is, **Erika Andiola.** Erika Andiola graduated from Arizona State University **(Forks Up!)** in 2013. She was a part of the Bernie Sanders campaign back in 2016 as a Latino outreach strategist. She focused on states in the Southwest and was also the Political Director for the organization **"Our Revolution."** "Our Revolution," also known as **"OR,"** is an American progressive political action organization that was formed out of Senator Bernie Sanders's 2016 presidential campaign.

At the age of 11, Andiola was brought over to the United States as an undocumented immigrant by her mother. She is using her past as a platform to help others in similar situations, struggling with immigration reform, just like she once did. When the United States Senate was contemplating on the **Development, Relief, and Education For Minors Act (The Dream Act),** Erika Andiola had come forward publicly as a Dreamer. She didn't have to do that, but she did. And she did it proudly. I admire her because, she is not ashamed of who she is and where she came from. Why should she be? She is a human being just like the rest of us, just trying to make a difference in the lives of others and, leave her mark on the world.

She co-founded the **Arizona Dream Act Coalition,** "which is an immigrant, youth-led organization, focusing on the fight for higher education and immigrant rights."[39] She did not use her past as an excuse to stay quiet and wallow in the pit of her own tribulations. Instead, she used her past as a reason to do SOMETHING about a reoccurring issue at hand. She sees the problem of immigration as her cause to fight and speak out against this social injustice. Andiola used social media, her school, and her own personal experience as a base to get her message out. This is a prime example of how we have multiple resources at our disposal, waiting to be used for something worthwhile.

---

[39] Wikipedia/Erika Andiola.

CHAPTER 7

"You must do what you think you cannot do." – Eleanor Roosevelt

I became fascinated with **Eleanor Roosevelt** after watching several **Netflix** documentaries on **President Theodore Roosevelt**, the **26**th President of the United States, and **President Franklin D. Roosevelt**, the **32**nd President of the United States. Eleanor Roosevelt, wife of President Franklin D. Roosevelt, first lady of the United States of America, was at first a background character in a much bigger picture that was centered around her husband and the politics, which was the center of their lives. From the beginning, Eleanor always struggled with insecurities about her personal appearance and even referred to herself as the "ugly duckling." Even her own mother referred to her as "Granny"because she was said to be *too* serious and plain. Beauty is in the eye of the beholder. I admire the strength and character of Eleanor Roosevelt. She did not let perceived imperfections about her looks deter her from her purpose.

Girls, we can learn from Eleanor Roosevelt. We must not get caught up in the vanity of this world. The opinions of others about our looks and our personality must **NOT** deter us from our dreams, our purpose, and the goals that we want to accomplish. Mrs. Roosevelt stated that "**No matter how plain a woman may be, if truth and loyalty are stamped upon her face, all will be attracted to her.**"

Eleanor Roosevelt had a strong desire of wanting her own identity. She wanted to be known for more than just being the wife of a President. She worked tirelessly, and pushed insecurities aside to become a public figure, a woman known for her humanitarian works. She was actively involved with the Red Cross organization and went on to achieve prolific acclaim for her work in **politics, education, social justice, and the well-being of others.** Although she came from a wealthy family, her life was not a cakewalk. There were many challenges, ups and downs, and fears, but she overcame them. She overcame adversity.

"**You must do what you think you cannot do.**" Eleanor wrote and lived by these words for the remainder of her life. Take heed to Eleanor's words and realize that challenges in life are inevitable, they are bound to arise. Nothing worth doing in life is ever easy and, if you give yourself a fighting chance by trying, you will go further than if you did not try at all.

Gen Zs, it is not uncommon that when applying yourself to new things, new challenges are bound to arise and cause dubious actions and feelings. **The key to achieving success is not giving up!** My mom often said this quote to me when there were times when I was doing something very challenging and wanted to give up. **"The scared don't try, the weak die along the way, only the strong survives."**

You should not go through life with a pessimistic, negative outlook on things and give up before even putting in an effort. When you do that, you're not giving yourself a chance to succeed. Be willing to go the extra mile, even when-at first- what you desire seems unattainable.

What obstacles did you overcome, because you did not give up?

_____

_____

_____

_____

_____

_____

S.L. Daughtrey

_____

_____

_____

_____

_____

_____

_____

_____

_____

_____

_____

_____

_____

_____

_____

_____

_____

_____

_____

_____

_____

_____

Write two goals that you want to accomplish within a year. Be specific. And, look at your written goals every day!

_____

_____

_____

_____

_____

_____

_____

_____

_____

_____

_____

_____

_____

_____

_____

_____

_____

_____

_____

_____

_____

_____

_____

_____

_____

_____

_____

_____

_____

_____

_____

_____

_____

_____

_____

_____

_____

_____

_____

Remember this. Sometimes you don't have to change your goal; just the plan.

Chapter 8

No Injustice Is Too Small If
It Impacts You

From a more personal point of view, I don't have any accounts where I have been wronged to the point where I was getting interviewed by "Ellen" or on "Good Morning America," nothing close to that. But there was this incident that occurred at the closing of my junior year, when I ran for Associated Student Body (ASB) Secretary at my school. It was my first time running for a position in office and, of course, I was excited because first, I was running with my best friend, and second, I thought I had a good chance of winning. When campaign week came around, I couldn't wait to hang my posters, well, at least one of them because one of the posters had a little letter design malfunction.

Anyhow, since this was my first year running for a position in ASB, I asked some of my senior friends—who either were still a part, or had been a part of ASB—for some tips that could be useful, or even "things-you-should-know" type of advice. So, when it was time for students to hit the polls, I was walking all over campus, trying to get people to the polls to vote. I was close to dragging them! All over campus with my best friend, adrenaline pumping, voice yelling across the foyer, saying, "Did you guys vote yet?"

And, of course, their immediate responses being, "Yeah!" or "I'm about to right now!" All the while, they knew that they weren't going to vote for me. They were just saying that to say it.

Campaigning is hard! People lie, saying that they voted but *really*, they were in the same place they were when lunch started. But I would walk over to get them anyway, just because I had a feeling they were lying, and majority of the time, I was right. People become apathetic, lazy! They fall into a false sense of security.

"Oh, she probably has a lot of people voting for her. My vote won't make a difference." And this is how sometimes the best candidate can lose an election. But what really warmed my heart was my friend, Devin, having the same energy that I had. He really wanted to see me win and was pulling his friends, and their friends' friends, to the polls with him, both days during the election! We had a strong sense of comradery. Especially, on the last day, when he brought a good crowd with him that I thought would bring me over the top for sure, and I needed those extra numbers because, despite knowing a large number of people, the more groups that we pulled in, the better the outcome would be.

We were purpose driven. It was frustrating at times, trying to get people to the polls. But it was worth it because I wanted to win. I believed enough people had voted for me. The election was a tough battle, and the votes were so close between the other candidate and me, that it resulted in a run-off, which was to be scheduled the following day. As run-offs began-run-offs being a further election process between two candidates that had the highest tallied votes in the previous running, I was anxious for it all to be over. Believe me, I wasn't arrogant about anything or thought that I had a for- sure win, I was just ready for the final results to be in, and in fact, I began to get a sense of foreboding because the turnout of those who had voted for me previously, was slow. It's as if they didn't think to come back to vote the second time when it was just as important! I called it apathy. People figured, "I voted once, I don't need to vote again, she'll probably win anyway."

And because my people didn't come out like they did first time, I lost. **It's not the will of the candidate that kills an election, it's the apathy of the people.** I am not bitter, but again I use the word—frustrated.

I vividly recall the moment I found out that I had lost. My best friend, Ivan, and I were the first ones at the ASB office after school. Even though he had already won the position he was running for, he was still as nervous for me, as he would've been if he were in the same position. When we got to the ASB office, the results hadn't even been posted yet, so we went inside looking for the girl with the results. I know, I know, "intrusive?" But, hey, I was anxious and ready to face the names on the paper.

When the girl with the results in hand walked past me and outside to plaster the results, I didn't follow because I felt stuck. All I knew was that I wanted to win and that I wanted to see the name, "**Shanaya Daughtrey**" under the title "ASB Secretary." When she was done taping the results, you could see the people already gathered around, frantically looking up and down at the paper to see if their names were on it. That wasn't me, I was still inside...waiting. Ivan, on the other hand, was six feet away from where I was and was able to see the names through the window. He moved closer towards the window and searched for my name with his finger. I knew my name wasn't on the list when he slightly put his hand over his mouth and kept reading it like it was magically going to appear. I also realized it when he hadn't said anything and kept looking at the paper, instead of turning to look at me. I had to see for myself, so I walked past Ivan to get outside, and realization hit when I discovered that my name really wasn't on the list. I kept staring at the name in the place where I thought mine would be, thinking the letters would magically rearrange themselves to form mine, but they remained the same.

As I turned to walk away from the name sheet, my best friend was beside me as we walked toward the gate to leave the school. No words came from my mouth, for I was trying to maintain a stoic, outward appearance because he knew I cared and I knew he knew that I cared, but I didn't want it to seem like I cared too much to the point where I was upset, but I was. I was upset and even his words of comfort didn't ease the agony of defeat that I felt.

From the ASB office to the gate leaving the school, I had only said two words to him before our departure from each other. My whole mood shifted. It affected how I was that day, all the way until the next day. I tried brushing it off. I tried not thinking about it, but how could I not?

I thought my chances at winning were solid! I thought enough people had voted to get me over the top. I was obviously wrong. When I told my mom that I had lost, she lectured to me about how next time I run for a position in anything, my way of campaigning has to be better. She was really adamant about team campaigning, meaning that it shouldn't just be two or three people, trying to help you get voters, but more to split up the workload. You should be willing to go the distance to see the entire process go through.

On a smaller scale, she was comparing it to **Clinton v. Trump**. In a way, our situation is similar. Not enough people turned out to vote and many were disappointed in the final results. But we are a democracy, and voting matters! Same thing with my election. Not enough people voted when it really mattered, so it ended up being someone else in the seat as ASB Secretary, instead of me.

That's life, though. Things don't always go our way and we have to adapt and look at what could be the next best thing. **Sometimes, we don't have to change our goal, just our plan.** So, in losing my election, I knew that there was another alternative to being a part of ASB. I could interview for an appointed member position. So, that's what I did. I made an appointment to be interviewed by the new appointed board so that I could still be a part of ASB.

The day before my interview, I wanted to have a good idea of what to expect before going in. So, I had asked one of my friends, who had been a part of the interview process before, and she basically said that the board asks you questions pertaining to "How would you balance your time with school, work and work for ASB?" "Why do you want to be a part of ASB?" Things like that. When I was told that, I felt ready, prepared to go in and knock the interview out of the park.

The day of the interview, I sat outside the ASB office, waiting for my name to be called. I didn't feel nervous or anxious because I was good at talking. Ask me a question and I can answer it fully. I did exactly that. The interview went great. So, when leaving the interview, I had no doubt in my mind that I was going to become an appointed member.

I waited two days for the results to be posted, and I didn't have the same feeling that I had when I was waiting for the results of the election because I felt confident that it was a done deal. I didn't feel anxious or uneasy about it, I didn't feel cocky either, but I did feel certain. The day finally arrived and, as I walked at a steady pace, ready to face the paper, there was no anxiety in my heart. I approached the window and was prepared to see "Shanaya Daughtrey" among the six names that had been chosen. To my complete and utter disbelief, my name was **not** on there!

It was a "WTF" moment. My eyes were literally glued to the paper in astonishment on how I was not among the six appointees. I was confused and started questioning everything I did in the interview. I asked myself, while going over the names again with my finger, "How did I not get chosen?" "Was my interview not good enough?" I asked myself these questions all the way up until I decided to go talk with the activities director in charge of ASB. He oversees everything that goes on in student council.

So, when I went to go discuss with him the decision of why I was not chosen to be one of the six appointees, he brought up election week, and how there was a discrepancy of my hanging around the voting polls when students were voting and that was a violation. I didn't think it was a problem because other people who were running in the election were sometimes hanging around the voting area, too. The question that came into my mind was, "Why was I the one singled out?"

I stewed on that question for hours. It was my first time running, I didn't intentionally hang around there just to break a rule that I didn't know existed, until it was brought to my attention. And that's what I told him. When I asked him why I wasn't chosen, he brought up how my being around the voting windows during the election, violated their code of conduct. That's what made choosing me to be a part of ASB questionable. He went on to say I was on a bubble of whether to be in or out. He said that the ASB President came to him because of the discrepancy and wanted a "bubble breaker" opinion, because the board was at a deadlock and didn't know what to do.

So, he being that person said, "If this is the reason why you can't decide to have her on the board or not, then she shouldn't be on the board, if she violated our code of conduct, then it should be obvious."

After being told that, I asked if there was a chance for a re-vote or a chance that my appointment could be reconsidered. He said it would be a 70% chance of a no, but that the ASB President could talk to him again about my appointment. I was still hopeful in that 30% leaving his office and I thanked him for taking the time out to talk to me.

As I walked back to class—dissatisfied with the way my conversation with the activities director of ASB had ended—I texted the ASB President, asking her if she could talk to him again about my appointment. When fourth period ended,

I ran into her in the hallway—thank God—and we talked about what led up to the decision to not have me on the board, and she mentioned how my presence around the voting windows was brought up and, I guess that action was frowned upon.

She did mention that there was some discrepancy—I know I've used that word a lot but, that's really what it was—and she personally wanted me on the board. She herself mentioned how great my interview was but didn't name the person who had brought up my being around the windows during the elections, which was understandable. However, she did go to talk to him and I thanked her before ending the discussion.

After school, I went to go talk to him to see whether the ASB President had gone to talk to him or not . She did but that hadn't changed anything. The 70% overruled the 30%. Before leaving I thanked him, and I walked that long lonely walk again to the gate of the school to meet my mom. It was mentioned that in the second semester of senior year I could run again, but I just nodded my head slightly and smiled.

When I got in the car I told my mom about all that had happened, and the decision that was made. Just like the activities director, my mom has a strong will, too. *Although she is very sweet, she can metamorphous into a purple lipstick-wearing bear.* She could clearly see that I was upset. It was obvious. She kept saying, "Next time do this," or "Next time make sure you..." You know, just tips for my next campaign...if I decided to go through that crap again. As she started dialing down on "Handy Tips From Mom," I brought up a point that I didn't think much of before. My mom was driving, and I said, "I really think it's messed up that I wasn't chosen to be a part of ASB just because I was hanging around the voting windows. I understand that it did violate their code of conduct, but I was never asked to leave like that other girl was."

As the car approached a red light, she came to a slow stop and turned to me with a puzzled expression on her face. She responded. "Wait a minute. The girl that was running against you for the same position was called out during election week for the same thing that caused a discrepancy during the discussion of your appointment, then resulted in you not getting picked?"

Without hesitation, I said, "Uh, yes." There was obviously something wrong with the whole scheme of how things went down. My mom just accentuated the fact that whoever brought up my being around the windows during the election week was **not** wrong. But the girl who was called out for the same thing, but didn't own up to it, during the time when I was being dismissed because of it, was indeed wrong, and that's where my mom saw the injustice.

Not long after leaving the school—mind you, we were now in the parking lot of Target—she called to discuss the issue with the activities director, who had the final say in the decision of my appointment. When she finally got in touch with him, she got straight to the point. Before even getting on the phone with him, she kept repeating to me how it's not just an issue of right and wrong, but an issue of **fairness**. And that was one of the main points that my mom was trying to get across to the activities director. Throughout what I heard during the conversation, he kept trying to steer the conversation toward the election and that I had lost.

My mom emphasized that it was no longer about who won the election, but what happened afterward, which was the interview to become an appointed member. And I explained to my mom that the interview was done by the four board members, who had just been elected. Among the four, I reminded her that the candidate who was running against me for ASB Secretary, was among those four who had the power to either "yay or nay," to my appointment. I was not trying to put all the blame on one person to change the outcome of the election, and neither was my mom, it was just the simple concept of **fairness**.

My mom requested a meeting with the principal to discuss the politics of everything. She was concerned with fairness and integrity. She believes that school leaders must demonstrate integrity and honor. She said, "In the realm of equality, cronyism and friendship have no place over doing what is right."

The meeting took place. According to my mom there were four people present: the principal, the activities director, my mom and the advocate that she hired on her behalf "to bring balance to the meeting." My mom described it as a productive meeting, and the principal was an excellent facilitator.

My mom, from the time I started school told me, "**Do not disrespect, argue, or cuss at a teacher.**" She told me that if there is ever a problem that I cannot handle or not being addressed after I talk with the teacher, counselor, or principal, to not hesitate to get her involved.

Because my mom went to bat for me and took action against what we both thought was unfair and unjust, the decision was reversed, and I ended up being a part of ASB. This whole incident just goes to show that people will only do you wrong, if you let them do you wrong. If I would have just sulked and brushed everything off, without vocally expressing what I thought was inequitable, then I wouldn't have been in ASB and the people in there would have gone on without a second thought about what had happened. Closed mouths don't get fed. You can't complain about something not going your way, when you don't make an effort to change the circumstances.

The incident was put behind us. We moved on and the ASB leaders and the appointed board members did what we are supposed to do. Make our school great!

CHAPTER 9

What Is Your Rosa Parks Moment?

What is your Rosa Parks moment? For some of you who may not know, Rosa Parks was a Civil Rights **icon**. Not giving up a seat on the bus may not seem like a big deal today, but back in her era, it could have cost Rosa her life. A good number of people think that Rosa Parks was the first person to resist bus segregation, and that's understandable because growing up and learning about civil rights in school, she was always the primary person that was highlighted when discussing the **Montgomery Bus Boycott**. All the attention started with Mrs. Parks, but she was not the first.

The National Association for the Advancement of Colored People (NAACP), considered her as the ideal person because she was already involved in the movement, she had a calm temperament, and a fierce determination for justice.

With Rosa Parks being an active and prominent member of her community, and willing to become a "controversial figure" of the boycott, her actions inspired other Blacks to boycott the Montgomery buses for over a year. To add some perspective, here are some statistics: **"40,000 African Americans participated in the boycott. They made up about 3/4 of the bus ridership in the city, totaling up to 90% of the city's African American population."**[40] That was a huge proportion of revenue no longer going toward bus transportation, meaning that the bus companies struggled and lost a lot of money.

With that in mind, the **Montgomery Improvement Association (MIA)** set out some demands that would be logical to comply to. The MIA was made up of black ministers and community leaders whose **"mission was to coordinate and maintain the boycott."**[41] But as a result of the city not wanting to comply with the demands set forth by the MIA, which were: **"To hire black drivers, to enforce courtesy, and have a first come, first serve policy."**[41] Blacks were forced to resort to other means of transportation to get around the city. But with the help of the MIA, carpools were formed, and even black taxi drivers rallied in, charging the same fair as the buses.

---

[40]study.com/Montgomery Bus Boycott

[41]study.com/Impact of the Montgomery Bus Boycott

Others simply walked to get where they needed to go. For the sake of change, fairness, and equality, African Americans were willing to give up riding on the bus, if that meant igniting change. In their hearts, they knew their sacrifice would be worth it in the end. You can't expect results if you're not willing to sacrifice and stand united. They were willing to sacrifice and stand united in the name of change, and as a result, on **June 5, 1956**, a Montgomery court ruled that the segregation mandate, violated the **Fourteenth Amendment**, deeming it unconstitutional.

There is no better feeling than knowing that you helped make a difference. Rosa Parks' moment began on a bus. The impact that she made, all by saying "No", was bigger than she could have fathomed.

My mom met her in person. She told me she stood in awe of having the opportunity to just be in the same room with this phenomenal woman. She also told me that one of her greatest treasures is her autographed book of *Rosa Parks Autobiography*.

There comes a point in everyone's life when you're going to say, **"Enough is enough."** It may be a national event that affects many, or it could be a personal event that affects only you. But, the one thing you know you must do is make a choice; only you can decide whether or not you're going to do something.

In most recent history, Malala Yousafzai—the youngest person to receive the **Nobel Peace Prize**—was shot in the head by a Taliban gunman on her way home from school on **October 9, 2012.** Her role as a young activist, advocating for girl's education, made her a target in Pakistan. Understanding the risks, she went against the Taliban, demanding that girls should be allowed to receive an education. She felt it to be her duty to stand up for people, who couldn't stand up for themselves.

All at the age of 17, she understood the value of education and fought for it, and was willing to die for it. Her unyielding belief in education is what gave her the courage to speak out against the Taliban and question their tactics of trying to take away her right to learn. In an interview on Pakistan television, she said, **"How dare the Taliban take away my basic right to education?"**

Voicing your opinion, on what you think is right, against a power force that is trying to instill fear in your heart, is not easy. But when is something worth fighting for ever easy? In 2009, at the age of 11, Malala, anonymously, began writing diary entries on the British Broadcasting Corporation (BBC) Urdu. She wrote about her life in her hometown of Mingora, under the rule of the Taliban, and how she yearned to remain in school and be educated. She also wanted other girls to have that same opportunity.

Even at the early age of 11, when most kids' primary worry was if they missed the latest episode of "Hannah Montana," she was worried about whether or not, she would be able to go to school and continue her education. *This just goes to show that it is never too early, or you're never too young*, to speak out against an injustice that affects you and the lives of others.

What is your Rosa Parks moment? Did someone accuse you of a wrong doing and you're afraid to speak out? Or you want to make a difference in the lives of others? For example, if you see an injustice—someone being **bullied** or you see someone being made fun of—do you hide in the shadows and say nothing, or do you engage to go along so you can get along?

I remember a time in elementary school on a mild spring day. It wasn't too hot and it wasn't too cold...it was just right. I had a good time in the classroom and at recess; tetherball went well that day. And for those of you who may have forgotten, tetherball was the game to play at recess. So, I was happy, and then things took a twisted turn for the worst. I went to retrieve my backpack, where I had lain it down near the tetherball courts, but when I went to get it, it was gone. I panicked, and started looking frantically for it. All my stuff was in there: my homework, my assignments, and my agenda. An agenda back then was a very important tool that we got graded on and counted as a large part of our grade in the class. As I stood there, tears began to well up in my eyes; I was dazed and confused. From the corner of my eye, I could see a figure walking up to me, and when I turned around, it was my classmate, **Syanne Patton.**

She had a concerned look on her face. She said, "Shanaya, I know where your backpack is. I saw who took it." A group of girls that I thought were my friends had hid my backpack. When I got home, I told my mom what had happened and how Syanne had told me where my backpack was. My mom said, "Syanne is a girl with courage, and she was not afraid to take a stand against wrong. I will always admire her."

My mom then emailed the teacher to request a meeting or she was going to go to the police to report a theft. She saw it as an act of bullying, and she takes bullying very seriously. She then went on to say that if it went unresolved, she would "hit the parents where it hurts—their wallets." Meaning that they would have to take time off work to go to court. My mom does not see bullies as victims, but potential criminals in the making. **However, she does believe that we must examine the root cause to find answers to what factors drive bullying behavior, and offer counseling assistance to the individual and lead the person on a path toward mental wellness.**

I thought it was over the top of threatening to get the police involved, but later on, I understood that if you don't stop bullying early, it progresses and only gets worse.

To this day, I often hear my mom repeat this quote, "**If you don't stand for anything, you'll fall for everything.**" She would often tell me "Shanaya, don't go along to get along. Choose to do what's right, because God sits high, but he looks low."

Unlike in the Wizard of Oz, you can't wish for courage.
The lion looked strong, but because he lacked courage, he had
a weak spirit. Instead of standing idly by witnessing a wrong
action, **Syanne Patton** demonstrated the action of someone
who is a drum major for justice!

What is your Rosa Parks moment? What will you do
when the time comes for you to stand up and say, "**Enough
is enough!**"

There will be moments in life, when we must decide if we
will do something about an injustice, or turn away and hope
nobody saw us run. Truth be told, we all throw shade; there's
no doubt about that. However, when it gets to the point to
where you are constantly belittling someone just for the fun
of it—with no regard for how that person is feeling and the
jocular remarks are no longer reciprocated in a comedic way—
is when the word "**bullying**" comes into account.

Stop And Think Right Now

Actually, think about and try to answer these questions,
not just read them and move on without a second thought.
Put some perspective on the questions listed below, and water
the seed that has now been planted in your mind. Don't ignore
what has now been brought to light. It's okay to question
yourself and your past actions. When perspective is put on
actions from your past, that gives you the opportunity to make

sure history does not repeat itself in your present, or future standing. I know personally, from both ends, how it feels to be the victim and sometimes the perpetrator. That doesn't mean I can't account for my wrongs and admit that at one time or another, I chose to do the wrong thing, instead of the right one.

1. What wrong doing have you witnessed and done, or said nothing?

_____

_____

_____

_____

_____

_____

_____

_____

_____

_____

2. How did you feel about it?

_____

_____

---

3. Did you think about what you SHOULD have done?

---

4. If given the chance, would you do things differently?

_____

_____

_____

_____

_____

_____

_____

_____

_____

CHAPTER 10

"The wisest man does not conquer the world; the wisest man defines time."
– Shanaya Daughtrey

What are you doing with the time that you have? How much time do you dedicate to making a change in the world in which you live? How much time do you dedicate to making a positive change in your home, in your school, in your community? Are you striving to be the best person that you can be? If not, are there steps that you can take to ensure the betterment of yourself? Are you actively working toward being a change agent as you go from adolescence to young adulthood? Or even young adulthood to adulthood and beyond?

24 hours equals 1,440 minutes, or 86,400 seconds in a day; so many opportunities to make a difference in your life,

or an impact on someone else's. Time should be valued, not wasted. It is one of the world's greatest commodities and we sometimes choose to consciously waste it on things that are not beneficial for us in the long run.

We're only human and we're young. So, there will be times where we get caught up in trivial matters. But, it's not okay when our life is filled with a lot of insignificant things, like gossiping and hanging out without a purpose. There are issues that we need to be concerned about right now such as: gun control, overpriced college tuition, and the effects of climate change.

Climate change is real-! Storms are getting more powerful. Ice caps are melting. Forest fires are becoming routine.

Wake Up, Zs! I believe that saving our environment will be the next **Civil Rights Movement** of our generation. My mom once said, "We must live in the present, learn from the past, and plan for the future." I don't know if she was the originator of the quote, or where the quote came from, but it's very poignant.

There's only so many hours in a day, and the hours that we do have should be spent on improving ourselves and trying to figure out how we're going to get from Point A to Point B, in a certain amount of time. Everyone's time is precious. Every minute can contribute to the betterment of yourself, how you want to live, where you want to be, and where you want to go. So even when you think that there's nothing to do, there is always something that needs to be done.

On a Wednesday during lunch at school, I was holding a meeting for my Toastmasters' Junior Club (public speaking for those who are not familiar), and at the closing of the meeting, one of my members had asked me why learning how to speak in public was so important. I went into detail, giving examples of historical and monumental events that were accomplished by people who were well spoken and were able to capture the attention of the audience.

My instant go-to example was the "**March For Our Lives**" rally. I told them how the student-led demonstration was a prime example of how being able to vocalize your words in a way that is comprehensible to others, is so powerful and meaningful that people are bound to listen. I went on to say other things about the way of the world and how being able to verbally express yourself is so vital.

In the midst of my minilecture, my Spanish teacher, who is the sponsor of my club overheard me. Her classroom was where we held our meetings. After the bell rang to dismiss us for class, I passed by her desk to say goodbye and to tell her to have a good rest of her day, but before getting to that, she stopped me. She told me how proud she was of me and how impressed she was by my maturity and world awareness.

I took the compliment to heart and thanked her repeatedly because I knew it was genuine and real. Upon returning from

Thanksgiving break, I had a club meeting on Wednesday. At the end of the meeting, my Spanish teacher handed me a charming little envelope with my name on it. She chuckled and admitted that she was supposed to give me the card before we had gone on break, but she forgot. We both laughed.

When I opened it to read it, I didn't expect a paragraph of gratitude. Tears started to form in my eyes as I read each line. Each word being meaningful and sincere. Up until that moment, I had no idea that my words about being able to vocally express yourself to the world around you, had resonated with her in such an impactful way. Her words made me realize that young people like us, really can inspire adults, not just people our age.

She thanked me for reminding her that teaching is a great profession, despite the difficult days that come with it. But she deserves a thanks as well because she revealed to me that my efforts in trying to be a mentor to my peers about the importance of public speaking and how your voice is a tool of the world, is not a waste of time, but instead the complete opposite. And that's what it is all about, using your time to either better yourself, and/or contribute to the growth of others.

So, thank you, Señora Acuna.

CHAPTER 11

We Have The Power

I talked about several great leaders in the previous chapters, now I'm going to talk about us. We have the potential to become great leaders, because I believe that in each of us, we possess a seed of greatness that God planted in us, and we must nurture and learn and grow so we could use our power in a positive way to help humanity. We can learn from those who came before us, we just have to minimize our fear, and even if we are fearful, it should not stop us from moving forward.

We have to realize that the world in which we live can sometimes be very harsh and brutal. When we fail, we shouldn't get discouraged, but instead fight to prevail. When life throws us a curve, we can't get lost in the midst of the chaos and lose our way. But things are only as bad as you make them, meaning that you are in control of your fate, you are in control of your actions and decisions. Most of you are probably familiar with the saying, "He was destined for Greatness," or "She was destined for Greatness." **"Greatness" is earned, not given.** In order to be great, you have to be willing to sacrifice and be willing to detach from your comfort zone. That takes will power.

Power is something that is in each of us, whether we know it or not and it can be a driving force that leads us to the top. What we do with the power that we have is up to us! **We are that acorn that can become a mighty oak!**

Now is our time, we have to be the ones to demand equality and justice. Closed mouths do not get fed, and closed mouths suffer in silence. No more having to suffer in silence when we have the tools to be heard! I have never personally experienced a major tragedy in which lives around me were taken without warning, so I can't say I understand the pain of people who have experienced it, or the survivor victims who lived through it. I can express sadness because it hurts when you look at the aftermath of a tragic event. That level of pain that a victim, or survivor, experiences reaches the depths of their soul. It cannot be transferred by osmosis and allows one who has not experienced such tragedy to say, "I understand your pain."

But, I do know that young people are dying every day from gun violence in the streets of Los Angeles, Compton, Watts, Chicago, Detroit, and other cities across the nation.

And it's sad; it hurts. When I watch the news today, and I hear people say,-(when violence strikes beyond the walls of the inner cities,) "I just don't get it. This is a good neighborhood. You wouldn't expect something as tragic as this to happen "here," or, "How could this happen in an area like this?"

For example, the response from some individuals being interviewed after the shooting in Thousand Oaks, California, November 14, 2018. News vans and reporters arrived, taking statements, trying to gather as much information as possible, and there was this one lady that I heard make this comment. "You just don't expect things like this to happen in an area like this…"

My question is, if not here, where do you suggest?

Why is it okay for shootings to happen in a place like Compton, or South Los Angeles, or East Los Angeles, but not in a place like Thousand Oaks? Is it because the majority of the population are Black and brown people? Why aren't the same amount of tears shed for the lives that have been lost in those areas? I am not trying to minimize the tragedy and pain that occurred in Thousand Oaks, California. I just want you to know this,

Hear Ye, Hear Ye! EVIL HAS NO BOUNDARIES AND IT TRANSCENDS COLOR LINES. And, AGAIN, IF IT SHOULN'T HAPPEN "HERE", WHERE SHOULD IT HAPPEN THAT IT'S DEEMED ACCEPTABLE?

Gen Zs, I cannot end this book without discussing the negative and sometimes tragic impact that bullying is having on our generation. We are now hearing on a frequent basis our peers committing suicide because they can't bear the pain any longer of being bullied. **WE HAVE THE POWER** to STOP bullying. **The statistics on bullying and suicide are shocking. Where is the outrage? The marches? The anti-bullying legislation?**

- Suicide is the third leading cause of death among young people, resulting in about 4,400 deaths per year, according to the Center for Disease Control (CDC). For every suicide among young people, there are at least **100** suicide attempts. Over **14** percent of high school students have considered suicide, and almost **7** percent have attempted it.

- Bully victims are between **2 to 9** times more likely to consider suicide than non-victims, according to studies by Yale University

- A study in Britain found that at least **half of suicides** among young people are related to bullying

- **10 to 14** year old girls may be at even higher risk for suicide, according to the study above

- According to statistics reported by ABC News, nearly **30** percent of students are either bullies, or victims of bullying, and **160,000** kids stay home from school every day because of fear of bullying.[42] I believe the numbers are higher, because, I do think it is under-reported.

In my Opinion, one Suicide is Too Many!

I asked my mom, who works for Los Angeles County Department of Mental Health, what happens to an employee who harasses another employee? First of all, she said, "**Prevention is the key.**"They have to do mandated trainings every year, or two. The goal she said is to create a "**non-hostile work environment.**"

I was totally shocked when she showed me what is posted at work sites. And, offenses are taken very seriously. They don't just say, "Oh, it's just adults being adults."

According to my mom, even if she overhears what she deems as offensive remarks or conversations, she can report it. Action will be taken. If children had these kinds of protections in place, bullying would not be a common occurrence in schools. And, children could be educated in a **non-hostile school environment. Maybe children should organize and form a union, too!**

---

[42] www.bullyingstatistics.org

THIS IS WHAT IS POSTED AT HER JOB SITE

How to Handle Bullying Cases and Article 39 Violations

VIOLENT ACTS

1. In cases of physical contact, **call 911.**

2. Document threats of violence, even if there are no immediate acts of violence,
   - File a police report within 24 hours.
   - File a Security Incident report.
   - Complete...

3. Document all physiological response.

   - Visit urgent care and get a doctor's note.

4. For additional COPING assistance, member may contact

   - Employee Assistance Program
   - Contact Steward, Member Connection, and/ or Work Site Organizer. An escalated grievance will be filed.

IS THIS BULLYING?

Bullying is present when there is a pattern of persistent, repeated mistreatment.
Categories of bullying behaviors include:

- **Physical: Spits, hits, pushes, throws, charts or instruments (Single or continued acts of violence should be reported under the Bullying charge.)**

- **Verbal:** Consistently gossiping about a worker with the intent to harm, shouting, swearing, name-calling, falsely accusing, demeaning, threatening to harm, taking down, being rude, insulting, humiliating, being offensive.

- **Nonverbal:** Intimidating body language, blocking a doorway, standing next to worker watching their every move, unnecessary following, isolating, excluding, sabotaging, consistently providing negative performance evaluations with no basis.

To Report Bullying or Discrimination:

Call Member Connection to report discrimination and/ or bullying.

Identify yourself as a **Bully Captain** or Steward.

1. Complete Article 39 Intake Form.

2. Determine whether bullying, discrimination, neither, or both processes should be followed.

   • Article 39 is for bullying...

   • ### is for discrimination.

   • General grievance process covers all other violations.

2. Work with Work Site Organizer/Steward to try and resolve the issue informally within your chain of command. Email Department Head and/or CEO to notify them of meeting and any other assistance you may need.

DISCRIMINATION – County Policy of Equity (CPOE)

Call ### intake specialist for discrimination cases based on: Gender; Religion; Age; Disability; Sexual Identity; Marital; Medical Condition; Race, ethnicity, or color; National origin or ancestry; Marital status

LOCAL 721, SEIU
Service Employee International Union

*(I did not include phone numbers or reporting numbers posted on the bulletin.)

Why can't we have these kind of protections in place on school campuses? Anti- Bullying Signs should be posted on the entrance of each school.

I often hear in the media from a certain politician proclaiming, **BUILD THE WALL!**

I agree. **LET'S BUILD A WALL!** Let's build a wall in Washington, D.C. that lists brick-by-brick, the names of all the children who have ended their lives as a result of unrelenting bullying.

Let's build the wall
starting with the names of:

McKenzie Adams: According to reports, a Black 9-year-old girl in Alabama allegedly took her own life after facing relentless bullying and racism in class. Relatives said she hanged herself December 3, 2018, in her room and was discovered by her grandmother. Since the start of the school year, the fourth-grader had been the target of bullying at US Jones Elementary School, where she was teased over her friendship with a white male classmate, according to her family. (https://nypost.com/2018/12/10/9-year-old-committed-suicide-after-classmates-taunted-kill yourself)

Kenneth Weishuhn (1997–2012): age 14, was a teen who is known for his suicide, which raised the national profile on gay bullying and LGBT youth suicides. Weishuhn, then 14 years old, was allegedly bullied in person. Death threats were sent to his mobile phone, and he was the subject of a Facebook hate group. He was targeted for being gay, having come out one month before his suicide.

Ty Smalley (1998–2010): age 11, was bullied because he was small for his age. Bullies would cram him into lockers and shove him into trash cans. They would also call him names like "Shrimp" and "Tiny Tim." On May 13, 2010, Ty was cornered in the school gymnasium and a bully started a fight by pushing him. Normally, Ty would just walk away when a situation like this occurred, but on this occasion, he stood up for himself and pushed back. He and the bully were both sent to the school office. **Ty served a three-day suspension, but the bully only served one day of his victim's suspension.**

Phoebe Prince (1994–2010): age 15, an American high school student, who died by hanging herself, following school bullying and cyberbullying

Tyler Clementi (December 19, 1991): was an American student at Rutgers University in Piscataway, New Jersey, who jumped to his death from the George Washington Bridge at the age of 18, on September 22, 2010. On September 19, 2010, Clementi's roommate, Dharun Ravi, used a webcam on his dorm-room computer and his hallmate Molly Wei's computer to view, without Clementi's knowledge, Clementi kissing another man.

Audrie Pott (1997–2012): age 15, a student attending Saratoga High School, California. She died of suicide by hanging on September 12, 2012. She had been allegedly sexually assaulted by three teenage boys at a party, eight days earlier, and pictures of the assault were posted online with accompanying bullying.

Jamey Rodemeyer (1997–2011): age 14, was a gay teenager, known for his activism against homophobia and his videos on YouTube to help victims of homophobic bullying. He ended his life by hanging himself, allegedly as a result of constant bullying.[43]

Angel Green hanged herself from a tree next to her school bus stop so that her bullies could see her in the morning. Early one morning in 2013, this fourteen-year-old from Indiana purposely hanged herself from a tree in front of her school bus stop so that her tormentors would see her lifeless swinging corpse.

---

[43]https://en.wikipedia.org/wiki/List_of_suicidesthathavebeen attributed to bullying

Rebecca Sedwick: In September of 2013, at the age of 12, jumped to her death from atop of an abandoned cement silo in Florida. Police who investigated her suicide uncovered abusive messages directed at Rebecca from a group of about fifteen girls at her local school. The girls had apparently been spurred by jealousy over Rebecca's former involvement with a local boy. These messages included, "Why are you still alive?" and "Go kill yourself."

Amber Cornwell, who was taunted by other girls because boys liked her, hanged herself after posting on December 20, 2014, "If I die tonight, would anyone cry?" on Facebook. Allegedly popular among boys at school and hated by girls because of it, this sixteen-year-old from North Carolina was an honor-roll student who played tennis and sang with the school choir. Despite what seemed like a bright future, her female antagonists insisted she had no future.

Megan Meier: A rival's mother invented a fake male persona on My Space to antagonize Megan, who killed herself after the "Josh Evans" character told her, "The world would be a better place without you."

WE HAVE THE POWER

TO CHANGE THE STAUS QUO

The Constitution Of Generation Z

We, the Young People of the United States of America, in order to form a more cohesive union, must stand on principles and work toward justice for all. We must ensure acceptance of our differences and strive to learn and grow in wisdom. We must stand on truth and challenge bigotry. Make no excuses, only changes, and strive to be the best that we can be to make way for a more humane and fair world.

E Pluribus Unum
Out of Many, One

WE HAVE THE POWER!

BIBLIOGRAPHY

Fall River Press (2002). The Constitution of the United States of America with the Declaration of Independence

(2016, January 24). Thomas Jefferson Retrieved from https://www.vocabulary.com/dictionary/ThomsJefferson

Wikipedia Contributors (Last Edited 2019, January 4). Retrieved from http://en.wikipedia.org/wiki/Mahatma_Gandhi

Wikipedia Contributors (Last Edited 2018, December 26). Retrieved from https://en.wikipedia.org/wiki/Report-to-the-American-People-on-Civil-Rights

Retrieved from https://www.thekingcenter.org/king-philosophy

Wikipedia Contributors (Last Edited 2109, January 6). Retrieved from https://en.wikipedia.org/wiki/EleanorRoosevelt

Cheprasov. A, Impact of the Montgomery Bus Boycott. Retrieved from https://study.com/academy/lesson/impact-of-the-Montgomery-bus-boycott.html

Retrieved from www.civiced.org/resouces/publications/resource-materials/constitution-of-the-united-states-of-america

https://nccs.net/

ikipe.southafrica.net/

Wikipedia Contributors (2019, January 4). Retrieved from https://en.wikipedia.org/wiki/Apartheid

(2018, April 2) Who was South Africa's Winnie Mandela. Retrieved from https://www.aljazeera.com/news/2018/04/South-Africa-Winnie-Mandela

Shortz, L. (2017, July 5). Transgender Bathroom Laws in California: What Employers Need to Know. Retrieved from https://www.mrllp.com/blog-transgender-bathroom-laws-in-California-what-employers-lara-shortz

(2018, April 23) Overview of State & Federal Gender Neutral Bathroom Laws. Retrieved from https://www.milrose.com/insights/state-and-federal-gender-neutral-bathroom-laws

https://www.aclu.org/video/truth-about-bail-it-doesn't-work

Wikipedia Contributors (Last edited 2018, November 25). Retrieved from https://en.wikipedia.org/wiki/Bail

Eckhouse, L. (2018, August 31) California abolished money bail. Here's why bail opponents aren't happy. Retrieved from https://www.google.com/amp/s/washingtonpost.com/amphtml/news/monkey-cage/wp/2018/08/31/california-abbolished-money-bail-here's-why-bail-opponents-aren't-happy/?

Wong, Curtis (2018, December 6) Kevin Hart's History of Homophobic Tweets, Jokes Resurfaces As Oscars Gig is Announced. Retrieved from https://www.huffingtonpost.com/entry/kevin-hart-homophobic-jokes_us_

Wikipedia Contributors (Last edited 2018, December 5) https://en.wikipedia.org/wiki/Stop-and-frisk_in_New_York_City

(2012, October 16) Winston Churchill-Prime Minister/ Mini Bio/BIO Retrieved from https://www.youtube.com

Taykor, J. (2018, January 4) How Churchill led Britain to Victory in the Second World War. Retrieved from https://www.iwm.org.uk/history/how-churchill-led-britain-to-victory-in-the-second-world-war

Wikipedia Contributors (Last edited 2018, November 19). Retrieved from https://en.wikipedia.org/wiki/Erika_Andiola

Ferris State University. Retrieved from https://www.ferris.edu/jimcrow/origins.htm

https://en.wikipedia.org/wiki/Chad_Griffin

TMZ (2019, January 7). Retrieved from https://www.google.com/amp/s/amp.tmz.com/2019/01/07/kim-kardashian-cyntonia-brown-clemency-tennessee/

About the Author

SHANAYA DAUGHTREY is senior in high school, currently residing in Southern California with her mom. She will be attending the University of Alabama in the fall of 2019. She plans to major in Political Science and her goal is to become an attorney, specializing in Constitutional Law.

ROLL TIDE!

**You can contact Shanaya at
sdaughtrey@icloud.com**

I Told My Story.

Now Tell Yours. Write Your Book! Starting Now!

_____

_____

_____

_____

_____

_____

_____

_____

_____

_____

_____

_____

_____

_____

_____

_____

_____

_____

_____

_____

_____

_____

_____

_____

_____

_____

_____

_____

_____

_____

_____

_____

_____

_____

_____

_____

_____

_____

_____

_____

_____

_____

_____

_____

_____

_____

_____

Generation Z

_____

_____

_____

_____

_____

_____

_____

_____

_____

_____

_____

_____

_____

_____

_____

_____

_____

_____

_____

_____

_____

_____

_____

_____

_____

_____

CPSIA information can be obtained
at www.ICGtesting.com
Printed in the USA
FSHW011127110319

9 780578 467108